CONTENTS

Assess yourself		03
1	Identifying your goals and your key skills	07
2	Preparing different types of CV	21
3	Winning with your CV	31
4	Making an impact with your covering letter	43
5	Researching the job market	53
6	Job-hunting online	61
7	Choosing the right first job	69
Example functional CV		77
Example speculative chronological CV		80
Where to find more help		84
Index		85

IMPROVE YOUR CV

EDITORIAL
MagBook Contributor Tommy Melville
MagBook Design billbagnalldesign.com
Digital Production Manager Nicky Baker

MANAGEMENT
MagBook Publisher Dharmesh Mistry
Production Director Robin Ryan
MagBook Advertising Director Katie Wood (katie_wood@dennis.co.uk)
MD of Advertising Julian Lloyd-Evans
Newstrade Director David Barker
MD of Enterprise Director Martin Belson
Chief Financial Officer Brett Reynolds
Group Finance Director Ian Leggett
Chief Executive James Tye
Chairman Felix Dennis

MAGBOOK

The paper used within this MagBook is produced from sustainable fibre, manufactured by mills with a valid chain of custody.

Printed at Polestar Stones

Improve Your CV
ISBN 1-78106-237-4

Assess yourself

Although CVs are only a part of the whole job-hunting process, they are normally the way you get to meet a potential employer and sell yourself face-to-face. This questionnaire is designed to get you thinking about your skills, and to give pointers about how to play up your strengths in your CV and covering letter.

Where you are asked to give a rating, think of 1 as the lowest grade (i.e. poor, very little) and 5 as the highest (i.e. excellent, very much).

1 Think of the five skills your potential employer might view as most important (if you are thinking of a specific job, the job description or advertisement should give you some ideas). Give yourself a rating for each skill.

....	1	2	3	4	5
....	1	2	3	4	5
....	1	2	3	4	5
....	1	2	3	4	5
....	1	2	3	4	5

2 Rate the match between your skills and your overall career goal.

1 2 3 4 5

3 Choose three of the following attributes that you think best suit you:

entertaining	team player	hard-working	intelligent
creative	eloquent	friendly	honest
serious	diplomatic	reliable	conscientious
professional			

Think how you can best introduce these in your CV or covering letter.

4 Make a list of any extra skills which may help you stand out from the crowd of other applicants. How would you grade yourself for each skill?

....	1	2	3	4	5
....	1	2	3	4	5
....	1	2	3	4	5
....	1	2	3	4	5
....	1	2	3	4	5

5 Rate yourself on each of the following interpersonal skills:

Communication	1	2	3	4	5
Assertiveness	1	2	3	4	5
Diplomacy	1	2	3	4	5
Negotiation	1	2	3	4	5
Teamwork	1	2	3	4	5

6 It's often useful to include a list of your IT skills. Rate your ability on each of the following:

Word processing (Word etc)	1	2	3	4	5
Spreadsheets (Excel)	1	2	3	4	5
Databases (Access, SQL Server etc)	1	2	3	4	5
Programming	1	2	3	4	5
DTP (Quark, PageMaker etc)	1	2	3	4	5
Internet	1	2	3	4	5
Website design	1	2	3	4	5

7 What is your main achievement of the past two years?

....

....

8 How could you relate this to the position you are applying for?

....

....

9 Think of the most important aspect of your education to date, and rate its usefulness to you in your job hunt.

1 2 3 4 5

10 Rate the experience gained from your spare time activities.

1 2 3 4 5

11 If you are thinking of changing career, think of the three skills you possess which could be most successfully transferred to your new potential career:

....

....

1

Identifying your goals and your key skills

If you've not written a CV (curriculum vitae) before or haven't updated one for a while, making a start can seem daunting. It needn't be like that, though, and some time spent in planning at the beginning before you put pen to paper or boot up your computer, will be time well spent. Don't worry yet about how to set out all you want to say and what style of type you want to use, but think instead about your 'marketable' skills—in other words, what will make you attractive to a prospective employer.

Most of us tend to think too narrowly about the skills we have to offer and as a result tend to undersell ourselves when we are looking for a new job or promotion. Here is a step-by-step guide to examining your life and work experiences, so that you can assess what your strengths are and 'sell' yourself more effectively on your CV.

Start by thinking about your personal and professional goals. What educational, career, and leisure experiences have you had that will help you in your future job? Do you have a realistic picture of the match between your skills and your overall career goal?

STEP ONE UNDERSTAND THE REAL PURPOSE OF A CV

A winning CV is not one that gets you the job—it is one that gets you the interview and so helps you get your foot in the door. Some people think that a fantastic CV alone will get them their dream job, but that is rarely the case. For most recruiters, advertising a job and asking for CVs acts as a preliminary 'sifting' process, whereby they can look out for the people with the right skills, experience, and suitability for a given role, and then fix a time to meet with them in person.

You need to create a CV that stands out from the crowd and that interests a potential employer enough for them to want to meet you in person. The employment market's never been more competitive, and a personnel officer or recruiter can receive hundreds of CVs for every job opening. Even if you're not applying for an advertised position, but are instead hoping to register with a job agency, you need to make sure that your CV looks impressive and well planned. Remember that you've only a few seconds to capture someone's attention, and you don't want it to be for the wrong reasons!

All of the above may sound daunting, but don't worry: the advice outlined below will help you put together the CV that you need to make a big impact, whatever job you're after.

STEP TWO BEGIN AT THE END

Your CV is your chance to advertise your most marketable skills. Preparing a list of these may seem like hard work, but it is well worth doing. This list will help you to write a more powerful CV, as well as to present yourself more professionally to a potential employer. It's also excellent preparation for an interview—you will feel confident about what you have to offer and will sell yourself better.

To best help you identify your marketable skills, you need to know what kind of a position you're looking for as it will help 'frame' your job search. This will make you focus on the skills that you will need in your next job. This is the time, then, to work out what you want to achieve in your future career.

Generally, people tend to submit **speculative** or **targeted** CVs. If you have just graduated, you are working but unhappy in your current position, or you were recently made redundant, then you are probably planning to contact a large number of potential employers in different organisations. In this case, you are conducting a general or speculative career search. In this case, you will need to use several different CV formats. For instance, if you have a background in both electronics and photography, you might have one CV that highlights your photographic skills for one set of employers, and another CV that highlights your electronics skills for another set of employers.

If, on the other hand, you are currently working and someone contacts you about a specific job opening at another company, or perhaps you learn about an opportunity for promotion within your current company, you are doing a targeted career search, and you should custom-design your CV to fit that particular job.

STEP THREE THINK ABOUT YOUR CAREER OBJECTIVE

Before writing your CV, you should have a very clear idea about which job you are looking for and the kind of company you would like to work for. If you are submitting a speculative application or registering your CV with an agency, you might want to include your career objective at the top of your CV, directly after your contact details. This will help people know exactly what type of job you're looking for.

Be as specific as you can. It's not enough to say, 'Seeking a middle management position in a dynamic organisation' (see below and opposite); you need to be clearer and describe your ideal job. However, make sure you don't go over the top and assign yourself a long list of impressive-sounding adjectives that are either untrue, or which you can't demonstrate in person. Be concise, clear, and honest.

Draft Career Objective:
Position in the broadcasting industry.

This statement is too general.

Improved Career Objective:
An experienced broadcasting professional is seeking a position that will make full use of an in-depth background as a television producer, production manager, scriptwriter, and networker. I am looking for a challenging production manager position that will enable me to use and expand my creative skills and international experience in the broadcasting industry.

Draft Career Objective:
Managerial position in a finance organisation.

This statement is too general.

Improved Career Objective:
A highly motivated professional is seeking a position that will fully exploit advanced education in managerial accounting and experience in all areas of finance and cost control. I have a proven ability to define key organisational issues, propose solutions, and implement changes.

STEP FOUR WRITE A BRIEF BIOGRAPHY

Now that you know what you are aiming for, sit down and write a detailed history of where you've been and what you've learned so far in your life. As you write about each experience, describe what you enjoyed and what you didn't enjoy, and what you accomplished. What are you most proud of? Then describe what you did when you were not working, and how you felt about those activities. Make sure that there are at least seven key events in your biography. Think about:

- Significant events when you were growing up.
- Educational achievements.
- Important life experiences, such as travelling, raising a family, caring for a partner or family member.
- A summary of your work experiences.

STEP FIVE REVIEW YOUR EXPERIENCES

1 Education

Use these questions to work out some of your skills and interests:

- Which teachers or lecturers did you like best and why?
- Which teachers or lecturers did you like least and why?
- Which subjects did you like best and why?
- Which subjects did you like least and why?
- In which subjects did you get the best marks and why?
- In which subjects did you get the worst marks and why?
- How have you furthered your studies since leaving full-time education? What motivated you?
- If you've recently decided to gain a new qualification or take up a new educational interest, what motivated you to do that?

Take some time to think about your answers to these questions and how they might relate to your job search and your skills. For example, if you found that, on reflection, you enjoyed classes or seminars that forced you to think on your feet or present your thoughts to large groups of people, you could be the type of person to flourish in a sales role. Whatever your findings, try to draw out five key skills, motivations, or areas of knowledge that you might like to use in your next position.

2 Work

Now think about your life thus far at work. Look back at each of the jobs you've had and ask yourself:

- **Which was my favourite job and why?**
- **Which was my least favourite job and why?**
- **Which of these jobs would I do even if I didn't get paid? Why?**
- **Which jobs really challenged me and helped me to develop personally and professionally? Why?**

Now identify five key skills or knowledge areas that you might like to use in your next position.

3 Leisure

What do you really enjoy doing with your leisure time (whether this is in the evenings or weekends, or during longer periods of time between jobs)? Think about:

- **What marketable skills have you developed from a hobby? For example, if you enjoy hunting in antiques markets, you may have found you've gained good negotiating or influencing skills from haggling with vendors.**
- **What skills have you developed from your travels? For example, have**

you learnt a new language or worked abroad?

- What skills have you developed from other leisure activities? For example, if you play sport regularly, have you found that you enjoy leading or motivating others as captain or vice-captain or your team? Or are you more of a team player who prefers a supporting role out of the limelight?

- Is there something you do for fun that you always dreamed of getting paid for? For example, if you enjoy spending time in your garden, would you love to design other people's gardens for them?

Again, identify the five most marketable skills you've gained from your leisure activities.

4 Other areas of your life

Many people today take career breaks to spend time looking after or raising children, or caring for ill relatives. Some of us need a change of scene after a particularly long or stressful project and go travelling for a while, or have to bounce back after a life-changing event such as illness, bereavement, or redundancy.

Even these very stressful experiences can provide us with helpful perspectives on life so think back over things that have happened to you and see how they've shaped your life and your goals.

For example:

- If you have a family, how has raising your children changed the way you do things? Have you found that you've strengthened your organisational or time-management skills? Have your priorities changed?

- If you have been a carer for a friend or family member, what strengths in your character has that experience brought out? Have you found that you are a good listener, or that you can motivate others when they are feeling low?

- If you've undertaken voluntary work, have you gained transferable skills or qualifications from that? What did you achieve in that work environment that makes you feel proud?

5 List your achievements

Now re-read what you have written and list at least ten major achievements in your life. It doesn't matter if they're not work-related. Then rank your achievements in order, from '1' being the most important achievement to '10' being the least important.

STEP SIX PUT EVERYTHING TOGETHER

1 Create a final 'skills inventory'

A 'skills inventory' gathers together all the key points you've discovered in steps one to five. To compile your inventory:

✓ List all your skills that are related to management. Don't be put off if your current job title may not say you are 'a manager'—some of your tasks may still be managerial in nature. These tasks can include:

- Making and implementing policies.
- Carrying out performance reviews.
- Hiring and/or firing staff.

- Managing projects.
- Solving problems.
- Managing budgets.
- Planning, organising, and presenting work.

✓ List any training you have done—whether as an individual or in a group, and including any informal training. Then list any qualifications you may have been awarded that enable you to teach classes in a particular subject. Include any other professional training courses or seminars you have attended.

✓ List all the times you have prepared reports or manuals, summarised research, conducted studies, and so on.

✓ List all your technical skills, such as operating machinery or computers. Include any specialised knowledge, any manufacturing, sales, engineering, personnel, or other skills that you haven't already mentioned.

✓ List all your interpersonal skills. Although some people find these hard to define, they can often make or break a job application. Interpersonal skills can include:

- Being able to communicate clearly and easily with people.
- Making things happen.
- Helping and instructing more junior staff.
- Getting people to agree to compromise if they have different points of view.
- Negotiation.
- Team building.

✔ Create a category of 'Other Skills' for any that don't fit into the above categories. Often, these skills are something unique that you have to offer, making you potentially more attractive than other candidates.

2 Compare the list with your career goals

By now you should have a good list of your marketable skills. Go back through your list and tick those skills that most closely match your career goals. From these ticked items, choose the ten that you think are the most marketable. Ask yourself, 'If I was trying to recruit someone for this job, are these the skills I would look for?'

Write a sentence to say how you have actually used each skill from your list of top ten. For example:

- Used conciliation skills to solve a major problem between production and sales.

or

- Conducted quality training in the finance department, leading to a 15% decrease in invoicing errors.

3 Do a reality check

Now, if you can, find someone who is doing the job that you would like to have. Ask him or her to review your list of skills and say if they match this kind of position. If they do not think there is a match, ask what skills you need to gain. Or you could ask what kind of a job would be a better match for someone with your skills.

Alternatively, ask someone close to you to you to review your skills and to see if you have left anything out. Try to find someone who you know will tell you the truth and offer constructive advice rather than blanket approval—while that's great to hear, it won't be helpful if it's not true.

STEP SEVEN GET READY TO MOVE ON

It's time to turn your list of marketable skills into key information in your covering letter and on your CV! The next chapters contain plenty of advice, information, and practical help on how to do just that.

COMMON MISTAKES

YOU DON'T THINK ABOUT YOUR OVERALL CAREER OBJECTIVE
It isn't a waste of time to think about what you've done, what you're doing now, and what you want to do next. Working out or just re-examining your career objective will mean that you can home in on the best skills you have or those that you need to acquire and transfer them to a CV that really does you justice.

YOU DON'T BOTHER WORKING OUT YOUR MARKETABLE SKILLS AND JUMP STRAIGHT INTO WRITING YOUR CV
You may think that you already know all your skills, but the exercise outlined in steps one to five always produces some surprising results that can help you market yourself better. Sometimes it even shows you that you may have chosen the wrong job objective. If this is the case, you can alter your career goals towards something that suits you better.

YOU DISCOUNT EARLY LIFE EXPERIENCES
You may believe that it doesn't matter what you did at school or in your first job—for some of us, it may be a long time ago now. However,

these early experiences often offer clues to your strongest skills and to where your real ambitions lie.

YOU'RE UNREALISTIC ABOUT THE MATCH BETWEEN YOUR SKILLS AND YOUR CAREER GOAL

You may want to change from working in information systems to a job in personnel, but without any training or experience in the new area, it won't be easy to make the leap. So make sure that you do a reality test before you actually start your job search.

STEPS TO SUCCESS

- Think about where you are now and where you want to be in a new position.
- Work out your career objective.
- Be realistic about how your skills match your perfect job.
- Be prepared to train or gain new skills to fill any gaps.
- Take the time to identify your main skills.
- Keep the information in your biography short and to the point.
- Be confident about your strengths and realistic about your weaknesses.

TOP TIP!

The steps described above will help you to identify the skills that will get you your perfect job. If you plan to change careers, don't worry: many of your skills will be transferable, or you may have skills that you haven't used for some time that could be very attractive in a new position.

- Look at all sides of your life for your skills: past history, education, leisure activities, life experiences, and current work.
- Think about those skills that can transfer from job to job easily.
- Talk to someone already in a similar job to check that you have appropriate skills, and that it is the job you imagine it to be!

USEFUL LINKS

- **Monster Careers Centre:** www.monster.co.uk

2

Preparing different types of CV

Now that you've spent some time thinking about what you really want to do and the fantastic skills you've got to help you get there, you can focus on transferring all that essential information on to your CV. There are countless styles of CV, but why do you need to know how to prepare them? Because every person's career history is different, and you want a CV that puts your career history in the most marketable and attractive light. When you apply for a job, think carefully about which style is most appropriate. A well written and targeted CV will impress a personnel officer much more effectively than a random story of your life.

Your particular job search and career goals are also unique. As you decide which type of CV to prepare, think about whether you plan on staying in the same field or whether you are changing careers. Have you had a fairly standard career development, or has your career been less traditional? Is this your first job? Are you aiming for a specific job in a specific company or are you on the look-out for something new and challenging?

All these factors will help you decide which type of CV is most likely to get you the interview that will lead to your perfect job.

STEP ONE CHOOSE THE RIGHT CV FOR YOUR JOB SEARCH

1 How many types of CV are there?

There is a wide variety of different types, but we will be focusing on the following:

- Chronological.
- Functional.
- Targeted.
- Capabilities.

A chronological CV is still the most popular type of CV by far, but knowing how to put together the other types will stand you in good stead as you progress through your career and come across different job opportunities. These days people may have several different careers (not just jobs) in the course of their working lives, so if you're thinking about changing what you do dramatically, a non-traditional CV may suit your needs best.

2 How do the CV types differ?

A **chronological CV** is ideal if you are staying in the same field rather than making a major career change.

- This type of CV also works well when you have progressed steadily up a standard career ladder. For example, if you began your career as a junior designer, you moved on to become senior designer, and you're hoping to become design manager, this is the CV type for you.
- You would also use this kind of CV when you have worked for the same company for most of your career, even though you may have had several different kinds of job within that company.
- If you are starting off on your career path, looking for your first or second job, this CV is probably most appropriate to your experience.

A **functional CV** is also a good choice when you are looking for your first professional job or when you are making a fairly major career change.

If you have changed employers frequently, followed a less traditional career path, or are concerned that your career history has been a bit patchy, you may be better off with this type of CV, as it focuses on your skills and accomplishments.

Use a **targeted CV** when you are very clear about your job direction and when you need to make an impressive case for a specific job.

It is hard work writing this kind of customised CV, especially if you are applying for several jobs, but it can make you and your abilities stand out from all the others in the pile.

If you are aiming for a specific job or assignment within your current organisation, you can use a **capabilities CV**.

Again, you must be willing to take the time to customise your CV for the situation.

3 Should I create a CV for each of these types?

Typically, no. The only exception to this is when you have created one of the standard formats (either a chronological or a functional CV), and a unique opportunity comes up where one of the customised CVs (either a targeted or a capabilities CV) would be better.

STEP TWO CREATE YOUR CV TO FIT THE SITUATION

There are some basic guidelines to follow when preparing each type of CV.

1 Chronological CV

- Put your name and contact details at the top.

- If you are applying speculatively, state your job search 'objective' clearly.

- Add your employment history. Start with your present or most recent position, and work backwards.

- For each position listed, describe your major duties and accomplishments, beginning with an action verb. Keep it to the point and stress what you've achieved.

TOP TIP!
If you've been working for some time, only write in detail about your last four or five positions, covering the last ten years or so. It's fine just to summarise the rest of your career history that goes back beyond that.

- Keep your career goals in mind as you write and, as you describe your duties and accomplishments, emphasise the ones most relevant to your desired job.

- Include your education in a separate section at the bottom of the CV. If you have more than one degree, they should be listed in reverse chronological order. List any professional qualifications or training you've undertaken separately.

2 Functional CV

- Put your name and contact details at the top.

- As this type of CV is well suited to people starting out in their careers, you may want to include a clear job search 'objective'.

- Write between three to five separate paragraphs, each one focusing on a particular skill or accomplishment.

- List these 'functional' paragraphs in order of importance, with the one

TOP TIP!

Using this CV style means that you can include information about your skills and accomplishments without identifying which employer or situation it was connected to. This is especially helpful if you've signed a non-disclosure agreement with your current or previous employer, in which you undertake not to reveal specific information about a job or project to potential competitors. Non-disclosure agreements are particularly common in high-tech or research companies.

most related to your career goal at the top.

- Provide a heading for each paragraph.
- Within each functional area, emphasise the most relevant accomplishments or results achieved.
- Add in a brief breakdown of your actual work experience after the last functional area, giving dates (years), employer, and job titles only.
- Include your education in a separate section at the bottom of the CV. Again, if you have more than one degree, they should be listed in reverse chronological order.

3 Targeted CV

- Begin by brainstorming a list of key points. For example, what have you done that is relevant to your target job? Are you proud of what you have achieved? Have you achieved anything in another field that is relevant to your target job? What do you do that demonstrates your ability to work with people?
- Put your name and contact details at the top.
- Think carefully about whether you need to include a job search 'objective' here; as this type of CV is best geared to an application for a specific job, you may not need to include one and could use the space more usefully.

- From your brainstormed list, select between five and eight skills/ accomplishments that are the most relevant to your target job. Make sure that the statements focus on action and results.

- Briefly describe your actual work experience beneath each skills/ accomplishment item, giving dates (years), employer, and job titles only.

- Include your education in a separate section at the bottom of the CV, listed in reverse chronological order.

4 Capabilities CV

- To develop a capabilities CV, you first need to learn all you can about the internal job that you are applying for. Then try to come up with between five and eight accomplishments that you have recently achieved that are relevant to this particular job opening.

- List your name and contact details at the top.

- Think carefully about whether you need to include a job search 'objective' here; as this type of CV is best geared to an application for a specific job, you may not need to include one and could use the space more usefully.

- Next, list your five top accomplishments, focusing on actions taken and results achieved that are relevant to the post you are interested in.

- Write a brief paragraph about any relevant work experience you have had in your current position. If you haven't been at the company for long, you should provide a complete synopsis of your work experience as described for the targeted CV.

- Include your education in a separate section at the bottom of the CV in reverse chronological order.

COMMON MISTAKES

YOU TRY TO INCLUDE EVERY SKILL, CAPABILITY, AND ACCOMPLISHMENT YOU HAVE

It's incredibly tempting to tell a potential employer everything you have ever done to try to impress them. A recruiter or employer will be looking for someone who can get to the point and express him or herself clearly and effectively, though, so remember to keep it simple and focus on those things that are most likely to get you an interview.

YOU DON'T USE ANY PARTICULAR FORMAT

If you haven't had much experience of writing CVs, you may create one that is a mixture of job listings, skills, and accomplishments. This will only confuse your reader. Rather than leap straight in, work out which type of CV suits your job search or your target vacancy best. Once you've done this, use the sample CVs at the end of this MagBook to help you with the final organisation of your material. If you're still concerned about which CV you think will suit you best, it might be worth visiting a career adviser. If you are still a student, your careers service should be able to help you for free. If you are working already, you'll probably have to pay for this type of service, and rates can vary quite dramatically.

YOU BECOME DISHEARTENED

Sales people have learned that you have to take a certain number of rejections before you get a 'Yes'. Finding a job is the same thing. If you receive a 'No' after making a phone call for an appointment, tell yourself, 'Well, that is one less "No" that I have to hear before I hear a "Yes".'

STEPS TO SUCCESS

- Think about the job you are applying for so you can choose the most appropriate CV to send.
- The most common types of CV are:

  chronological: when you are staying in the same type of work.

  functional: when you are applying for your first job, or for when you have a varied work history.

  targeted: when you know exactly what job you want.

  capabilities: when you want a job within your current company.
- As far as possible, each time you send your CV out, customise it so fits in with the job you're applying for.
- Don't waffle! Include only relevant information, but take care to explain yourself clearly.
- Follow up anything you have said you will do, such as calling to make an appointment.
- Don't be put off by rejection. It just means you are one step closer to a 'Yes'!

USEFUL LINKS

- **Total Jobs:**
www.totaljobs.co.uk

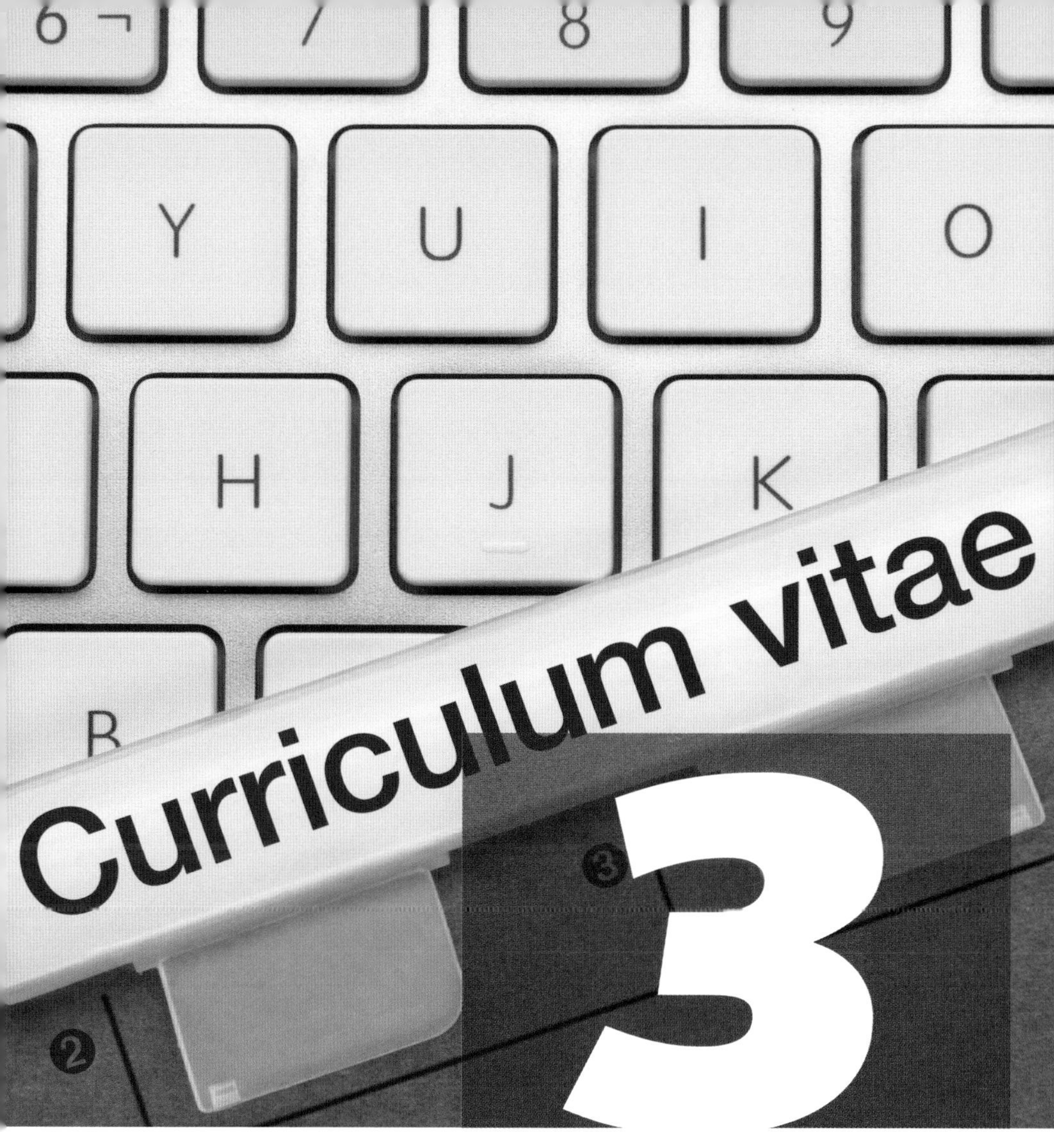

3

Winning with your CV

The planning process is over now, and it's time to create the ultimate marketing tool—the CV that will help you get the interview you want.

STEP ONE GET BACK TO BASICS

The steps described here are particularly helpful for anyone creating a CV for the first time, but they are just as useful when thinking about how you might update and improve your current CV.

1 Select your CV type

Decide on the best type of CV for your particular background and career goals. Chapter 2 explained the different types of formats available to you, but in this chapter we'll use a standard chronological CV as an example.

At this stage, also think about the optimum length for your CV. Two pages is fine: it's hard to get across anything useful in just one page, but a CV that is more than three or four pages is far too long and will give the impression that you can't focus or get to the point.

Don't worry if you're a recent graduate—prospective employers still want to know about your achievements.

Naturally they're particularly interested in work experience you've gained, but even musical or sporting achievements will show that you are tenacious and focused.

2 Revisit your career objective statement

Remind yourself about how to create a career objective (p. 10). Make sure your objective still holds true as you compile the different strands of your CV.

STEP TWO ORDER THE INFORMATION ON YOUR CV

1 Plan what you want to say

Now's the time to think about the headings you're going to use and the way you're going to order the information on your CV.

The three major categories of information in a typical chronological CV are:

- Contact information.
- Career history or work experience.
- Education.

If you think it's appropriate for your job search, you may also want to include your 'career objective statement' after your contact information.

✓ **Begin your CV with information about you and how people can get hold of you if they'd like to invite you for interview. List your name, address, contact phone numbers, and e-mail address if you have one. Don't use your existing work e-mail address: it may look as if you're taking**

> **TOP TIP!**
> Remember that your CV is not a life history. You should include information that is most relevant to your reader, the recruiter, rather than including everything you can possibly think of.

advantage of your current employers. (You also run the risk of your current employers finding out about your job search.) Use your personal e-mail address at Hotmail or Googlemail, for example.

✓ Decide whether your career history or your education is the thing that makes you most marketable. If you are just graduating from university and have not had a lot of professional experience, then you need to highlight your educational achievements first. If, on the other hand, you've been working for some time and have gained skills or experience you want to draw attention to, put your career history first.

Other categories that you might then include in your CV are:

- Academic achievements.
- Fields of study.
- continuing education.
- Professional achievements.
- Advanced training.
- Professional affiliations.
- Computer expertise.
- Other interests.
- References.

2 Write something for each heading

Listing educational accomplishments is very straightforward and involves giving details of:

- **Any courses, qualifications, or degrees you have completed or are studying for.**
- **When you completed or are aiming to complete the course(s).**
- **The name and brief address details of the educational establishment at which you took, or are taking, the course(s).**

If you are taking or have completed any professional qualifications, list them in the same way.

Reporting on your professional experience can be much harder, though. To communicate where your expertise lies and to emphasise your achievements, try to begin the statements in this section of your CV with an action verb and include measurable results as far as you can. For example:

> **Designed and developed an ISO-9001 programme that led to a 19% increase in international sales.**

or

> **Managed a 300-bed healthcare facility and improved patient satisfaction ratings by 24% over two years.**

or

> Liaised with key in-house staff and an international team of freelances to deliver a complex project on time and £10,000 under budget.

Some people decide not to include information about their other interests (such as sport, travelling, hobbies and so on), but if those interests are important to you, it's no bad thing to include them on the CV—it will give you an opportunity to show a 'fuller' picture of yourself, and also gives the interviewer something to discuss if he or she wants to break the ice or just find out more about you.

> **TOP TIP!**
> Don't include 'socialising' as one of your other interests if you include them on your CV. You can just about get away with it when applying for a place at university or college, but your CV isn't the place for that type of information!

Similarly, some people choose not to include information about their references on their CV. If you'd rather disclose the contact details of your referees at a later point in the selection process, simply write 'References on request' at the end of your CV as the final heading. If you do want to include your referees on the document, make sure you have their permission to do so before your start sending your CV to recruiters.

STEP THREE WRITE IT!

1 Fit the information together

You've decided on the career search you're undertaking, you've worked out your career objective, and you've assessed your skills. Now you need to lay out all that experience to best advantage and catch the recruiter's eye.

As a general rule, bear in mind the overall visual impression of your CV—include as much white space as you can so that your CV is attractive and the text uncramped. Also bear in mind the following.

Content

Don't lie about your qualifications or achievements. Remember, a CV is a way to secure an interview rather than a ticket to an instant job offer, so you must be able to back up claims you make on your CV. Very often you may be given a test as part of your interview (or even an online test before an interview), so if you say you have skills or proficiencies that you won't be able to demonstrate in a test situation, it will be embarrassing for everyone involved. Be proud of the skills that you do have, and make the best use of those. Also, once a person has been appointed to a position, his or her CV goes on the company's file, so there will always be a record of what you said you can do that can be compared with what you really can do.

Customise your CV. There are lots of books and Internet sites that will offer CVs for every occasion, but be wary of following examples slavishly and remember to bear in mind your 'target audience' at all times.

Explain gaps in your career history. If you went travelling for six months or took a career break to raise your family, say so. You don't need to give into lots of detail (particularly if you or a family member have been unwell, say), but wherever possible, stress what you learned in your time out, whether it be new language skills or a talent for organisation. Don't be embarrassed to explain if you were made redundant at one point in your career. Many people are affected by redundancy at one point or another and it is rarely a reflection on you, your skills, or your capabilities.

Look and feel

Most CVs are submitted via e-mail these days, but if you are asked to send your CV by post, print the document on high-quality white or cream paper. This will make sure that your CV can be easily read, photocopied, or scanned by the recruiter.

Buy your own stationery. Don't use headed notepaper or address labels from your current place of work when you are printing out or posting your CV to another company or agency. Just like using your work e-mail as part of your contact details, this will give a strong impression that you are taking advantage of your present employer's facilities.

Take care with the formatting of your CV. Use a 'clean' looking font that is easy to read (some people prefer a sans serif, such as Arial), and make sure that the type size you use isn't too small. Draw attention to your achievements by using a bold face to highlight positions you've held or qualifications you've gained. Emphasise key points in lists by using bullets.

Make sure you read over your CV once you've finished working on it to check for spelling or grammatical errors—these, above all, will mean your CV ends up in the bin rather than on the right person's desk. It's always a good idea to ask someone else to read over your finished CV too; he or she may spot something you've overlooked as you've become so familiar with what you've written.

Try not to rely on computer spellcheckers. While they will pick up on a good deal of mistakes in spelling and usage, remember that they won't pick up on words that are spelt correctly but used in the wrong way or the wrong place. For example, if you write 'there' when you actually mean 'their', the spellchecker won't realise that you've made a mistake.

✔ Unless you're specifically asked by a recruiter to submit a hand-written CV or covering letter, use a computer to give a professional finish.

✔ Follow your own instincts. While a second opinion on your CV is valuable, if you ask 20 people what they think, you'll get 20 (probably different) opinions. In the end you are the one who needs to feel comfortable with it.

2 Follow up if appropriate

When you send your CV out, you may want to follow it up with a phone call. If you have sent a speculative application to a company, it's fine (and in fact shows initiative) for you to get in touch with the person to whom you sent your CV to check that it arrived safely and to see if you can fix an appointment to meet them in person.

If, however, you submitted your CV in response to an advertised vacancy, it's not always advisable to telephone to try to arrange an interview. The recruitment process can take a long time, and managers may not respond well to what they might feel is a nagging phone call. Naturally if you've not heard from a company for some months it's a good idea to contact them then to find out what is happening, but use your common sense and try not to call too soon.

3 Keep it up to date

Aim to update your CV at least once a year, even if you are not actually looking for a job. Try to add any new achievements or skills as they occur or you may forget them.

COMMON MISTAKES

YOU SEND AN OLD CV BECAUSE IT'S ALL YOU'VE GOT
Don't be tempted to submit an ancient CV when you spot an advert for your dream job out of the blue—if you wrote it five years ago, it won't really represent who you are now and all you've achieved in the meantime. Take some time regularly to update your CV to reflect changes to your job title, your role, any qualifications you've gained or are studying for, or even a pay rise. You'll be less likely to be caught on the hop and you'll be able to react more quickly to new opportunities.

YOUR CV IS TOO 'BUSY' AND HARD TO READ
You may think that recruiters want as many details as possible about potential candidates who apply for a vacancy, but they really just need to know quickly if you have the basic qualifications and experience for it. You're making their job more difficult if your CV has long sentences, complex paragraphs, and has too many words on the page. It's better to have a spacious and easy-to-read two-page CV than a crammed and dense one-page CV. Make your CV visually appealing with lots of indentations, and with lines inserted between sections. Try not to use more than two different fonts and more than three different type sizes—they'll just detract from the content of your CV.

YOU OVERSELL
Don't be tempted to make what might seem to be boastful or arrogant claims in an attempt to grab others' attention. Instead, back up what you say with measurable results. It is much better to let your achievements speak for themselves.

STEPS TO SUCCESS

- Think about whether your CV is for a targeted or a speculative career search, as this will affect what you include and how you present it.
- Plan your career objective carefully, and be clear and precise.
- Map out your CV in rough first, thinking about the order of the information you will include.
- Don't write your life story. Keep to the point and keep your target reader in mind.
- Make sure you present your CV professionally and legibly.

USEFUL LINKS

- **Monster Careers Centre:** www.monster.co.uk
- **Total Jobs:** www.totaljobs.co.uk

4

Making an impact with your covering letter

When you send in your CV to a manager or recruiter to apply for an advertised vacancy or to let him or her know that you are looking for work, you'll normally send a covering letter too. 'Letter' is a bit of a misnomer these days as the vast majority of CVs are submitted by e-mail, but the principles are the same and we'll use the phrase to cover print and online versions in this chapter.

If you're applying for an existing vacancy, your covering letter should briefly describe the position you're applying for, where you saw it advertised, why you are particularly qualified for the job, and why you want to work for that specific company. If you're approaching an agency to register your CV as part of your search for a new job, you should describe the type of job you're looking for, the skills you have that would make you an attractive candidate, your current salary, and any preferences you may have in terms of location.

In all cases, a good covering letter can give a sense of who you are that may not come across in a CV. When you come to write your letter, remember to think about its tone, how you are describing yourself and your skills, and also remember to include the results of any research you've done into the company or field of work you're interested in.

If you sound both interesting and interested in your covering letter, you are much more likely to get noticed, interviewed, and employed!

STEP ONE UNDERSTAND WHY A COVERING LETTER IS IMPORTANT

The covering letter is the very first thing a recruiter or manager reads. It must grab his or her attention and make him or her want to read your CV and meet you. It is your first chance to stand out from the crowd.

There are a variety of reasons why you might write a covering letter and send a CV. These include:

- **Responding to an advertisement.**
- **Following up on meeting someone.**
- **Letting a potential employer or employment agency know that you are available for work.**

Other situations may well require a different approach. For example:

- **When you send a letter to enquire whether there are any job openings. In this letter you would ask who you should send your CV to.**
- **If you visited an organisation in person and filled in a job application.**
- **When you apply for a job on the Internet. If you apply online via an agency, you may be asked to fill out a form to accompany your CV attachment. Often you'll just be asked to give your contact details, but some agencies ask for a brief supporting statement to accompany your CV.**

TOP TIP!

One way of making an immediate good impression is by addressing your letter to a particular person. Letters that are addressed to 'Dear Sir/ Madam' or 'To Whom It May Concern' are usually thrown away. Most adverts will give a contact name, but if not, ring the company to find out or check on their website.

If you are replying to an advertised job vacancy, a covering letter also gives you the opportunity to include details that the advertisement may have asked for but which can't easily be fitted into a CV format. These could include:

- What attracts you to the job.
- Current salary.
- Desired future salary.
- Notice period.
- Preferences for geographical location.
- Dates you may be available for interview (you may want to include these if you are about to go on holiday for a while).

STEP TWO DRAFT THE LETTER

1 Say why you're writing

If you are applying for an existing vacancy, begin your letter by describing the position that interests you and explain why you are writing in the first sentence. You could also say where you saw the vacancy. For example:

> I am very interested in the position of Production Manager as described in your advertisement of 19 September on the *Daily Post* website.

Alternatively, if you're writing following a recommendation from someone already working at, or known to, the company:

I have been given your name by Jane Robertson regarding the position in Human Resources.

2 Show that you're interested

Take time to show that you've done your homework and that you understand what the company does and what its aims are.

TOP TIP!
You will conduct a more successful job campaign if you combine well-written letters with effective face-to-face and telephone networking.

✔ Visit the relevant company's website and look at any recent news articles, especially its press releases.

✔ Read relevant business newspapers and trade magazines. These will give you a sense of any industry issues facing the company you are interested in. They may also have particular information about the goals of your target company.

To get across the fact that you've read thoroughly and understood the job advertisement, match the language you use in your letter to the advertisement itself. For example, if the job description mentions 'team leader', refer to that job title rather than using the word 'manager'.

TOP TIP!
The Internet is a fantastic research tool, but make sure you bookmark relevant sites or articles so that you can find them easily if you're asked to an interview.

3 Tell them why they need you

Describe your qualifications early in the letter to grab the interest of the personnel officer or manager. Explain how your qualifications will help the organisation achieve its goals. For example:

I understand that your company is planning to relaunch its Web presence to support your sales. In my current position as Director of Internet Sales for Speedy Sales Company, I have helped to increase our market share by 13% in the past year.

Show how you and you alone can help this company deal with any challenges it faces.

4 Suggest an interview

You can do this by saying that you are going to be in their area at a particular time and that you would be available for an interview. Or you can simply say, 'I look forward to discussing how my qualifications can help your organisation to be more successful.'

STEP THREE REMEMBER THE ESSENTIALS

- ✓ Keep your letter short and to the point. An effective covering letter is usually only two or three paragraphs long.

- ✓ Be yourself. CVs are factual records of your experiences and skills. A good covering letter is your chance to show your personality and stand out from the crowd of other applicants as the interview short-list is drawn up. Keep the letter professional, but don't be afraid to show your enthusiasm, your willingness to work hard, and your interest in the position. Potential employers want job applicants who show an interest in them and who seem eager to be a part of their company.

✔ Make sure your covering letter looks professional. Check that there are no grammatical or spelling errors, and read it carefully before you send it off. If possible, ask a friend to check it for you too. Triple-check that you have spelled correctly the name of the person you're writing to.

✔ Use a standard and easily readable font such as Times New Roman or Arial.

✔ As with your CV, if you are submitting by post, use the highest quality paper that you can afford. Also, unless you are applying for a particularly creative post, use a plain coloured paper in ivory or white.

✔ Send any requested hard copies in a large flat envelope. You may want to send two copies in case the recruiter needs to show your letter and CV to different people, and photocopies or scans will be clearer if the originals have not been folded.

✔ If you are e-mailing your covering letter and CV, remember to check that you've attached the files before you send the e-mail! Also tell the recipient what type of file you're attaching and be prepared to send it in another format in case they have difficulty opening it.

COMMON MISTAKES

YOU USE A COVERING LETTER TEMPLATE FROM A BOOK
Reading through examples of covering letters in books can help you to understand what to include, and the layout and tone of this kind of letter. However, you must remember to change the letters to fit your needs. Most managers will have seen hundreds of covering letters and will not want to hear the same old phrases. Personalise each of your covering letters so that they are targeted at a particular person and company, and so that they represent you and your uniqueness. Some people literally 'fill in the gaps', and write a generic covering letter that they 'customise' by hand-writing the recipient's name and their own signature. Avoid at all costs.

YOU USE THE SAME COVERING LETTER FOR ALL YOUR JOB APPLICATIONS
A covering letter is meant to show that you really want to work for one particular company—taking the time to write a personal, company-specific letter will make all the difference to the impression you give! Using the same covering letter for all your applications also increases the likelihood of you making mistakes when you're tired or in a rush—you may inadvertently mention the wrong company in the body of your letter.

YOU DON'T FOLLOW UP
This is the commonest and most serious mistake. If you said you would phone to set up an appointment in your covering letter, you must note the date down and follow it up. Judge the situation carefully, though, and only contact the recruiter if appropriate. See p. 39 for more information.

STEPS TO SUCCESS

- Tailor your letter to the company and/or person you are applying to.

- Do your homework and research the company: the Internet has made this much easier, so there's no excuse for not doing this.

- If the company's website doesn't have the information you need some promotional literature, such as a catalogue or annual report, might.

- Keep your letter short and to the point.

- Show how your experiences and qualifications will help the company directly.

- Be polite, enthusiastic, and confident in your abilities.

- Use good quality paper (if you're asked to send hard copies) and a clear font.

- Proofread everything carefully before sending it out, and ask someone else to read over it as a final check if you can.

- If you're replying to an advertised vacancy, check that you've given all the information that the advertisement requested. For example, if the recruiters want to know your current salary and notice period, make sure you've mentioned them.

USEFUL LINKS

- **Prospects:**
www.prospects.ac.uk

5

Researching the job market

A great CV and covering letter are key parts of your job search, but to use them to best effect you need to collect together different types of information as well.

To find the right job and present yourself in the best possible light at interview, you'll need to research industry trends and find out as much as you can about the companies you want to work for.

Keep the following questions in mind as you start your search:

- **Where can I find out extensive and accurate information about the companies I am interested in?**
- **What kind of information do I want to know about each of these companies that will help me to write a covering letter that gets me noticed and to perform well at interview?**
- **What do I need to know about the industry I want to work in that will help me to ask and answer intelligent questions?**
- **What is the most efficient way I can find and save this information?**

STEP ONE DO THE RESEARCH

1 Start broadly: research industry trends

In the early stages of your research, you should begin by researching industry trends. If there's a good library nearby, ask the reference librarian for help in finding reference guides and publications containing information about industry trends.

In a nutshell, you need to look out for:

- Major growth areas.
- Major and up-and-coming players.
- Key challenges, opportunities, or potential problems for a given industry.

2 Use the research to pin down what you want to do

If you are not sure which industry you want work in, there are several good references and reports on attractive jobs and desirable companies. Look at the Financial Times website (www.ft.com/companies) and the UK Trade and Investment website (www.uktradeinvest.gov.uk) which provide well-organised information about trends in various business sectors. The Economist website contains business briefings by country (www.economist.com/countries). Look also at the websites of the top business schools—these give guidance on where to go and which directories to look at. Get some professional help if you need it: a lot of information will be available online, but it can be difficult to pull it all together.

TOP TIP!
Researching the job market thoroughly will give you a clear idea of what kind of work attracts you. The information you gather will help you design a more effective CV and to write an intelligent covering letter.

STEP TWO GO FROM A MACRO TO MICRO LEVEL

1 Research your chosen companies

The next step is to narrow your research by gathering information about the companies you would like to work for. Aim to find out:

- The size of the organisation (sales, profits, market share, numbers of employees).
- Its mission statement.
- The company's strong and weak points.
- Its key partners.
- Its key competitors.
- Information about the organisational culture.
- How the company is organised.
- Its key strategic challenges.
- The subject of recent press releases.

The vast majority of companies have websites these days, so it's relatively easy to get your hands on all this information. If the company you're interested in doesn't feature this information online, though, or you don't have access to the Internet, use your local library, where your librarian should be able to find you business reference guides that provide background information on specific companies. One of the most popular guides to company information is the Kompass Register (www.kompass.co.uk). Once you have found an organisation that you are interested in, get hold of a copy of their annual report. Download it from their site or phone them and ask them to send you a copy.

TOP TIP!
Read annual reports from back to front: the important information, such as the facts and figures on how the company's really doing, will be at the back. The glossy PR pages are at the front.

2 Speak to current employees

If the company you're interested in is based near where you live, see if you can find a way to talk to some of the employees—you may have friends in common. They'll be able to give you a good idea of what it's really like to work there.

TOP TIP!
If you can't get to know someone who works at your target company, see if your local chamber of commerce can help (www.britishchambers.org.uk).

STEP THREE THINK ABOUT THE JOB YOU WANT

1 Research information about a specific job

When you are looking for a specific job in a specific company you will want to know:

- What qualifications are needed?
- What would my tasks and responsibilities be?
- What is the typical salary for a job like this?

Most of these questions will be answered in your interview, but if you can gather information ahead of time, you will be better prepared for your covering letter, your CV, and your interview. If the job has been advertised, then the tasks and responsibilities will have been listed. If you know for sure that there is a job opening, ask the company to send you a copy of the job description.

2 Match the time you spend on research to the position

If you are seeking a very high level executive position in the same industry, you may already know most of the information listed above. If you are seeking a high level position in a new industry, you may need to spend several weeks on your job market research. If you are seeking a specialised position, you may not need to know as much about industry trends, but you should do several days' research on your chosen organisations.

TOP TIP!

Spend time researching industry trends to help you decide whether you want to stay in your current field, or whether you'd like to move to something entirely new. If the trends show that you are in a declining industry, it may be time for a change. Also, when you have an interview, your research will help you to ask informed questions.

COMMON MISTAKES

YOUR RESEARCH IS PATCHY

If you don't thoroughly research the industry, the company, and the job, gaps in your knowledge if you get to interview may jeopardise your chances. If you can demonstrate that you have done your homework, you will stand out from the crowd and will have a better chance of being offered the job.

✗ YOU DO SO MUCH RESEARCH THAT YOU CAN'T KEEP TRACK OF IT ALL

Create files for each of the industries and companies that you are researching. Organise the information so that you can find what you need quickly— especially important when you are preparing for an interview. You could make a set of index cards listing key points that you want to remember. Carry these cards with you and look at them when you get a spare minute to help you learn and remember important information.

STEPS TO SUCCESS

✓ For your chosen industry, find out the major growth areas, the major players and the major challenges and problems for this industry.

✓ Find business reference guides and publications online or in your nearest city or university library.

✓ Keep your research broad at first, then narrow it down to a few companies you would like to work for, then find out all you can about one chosen company.

✓ If you have chosen a local company, ask friends or family members if they know anyone who works there. Speak to existing employees if you can about the company culture, competitors, and any challenges the company faces.

✓ Organise all the information you have gathered so that you can find it easily.

✓ Match the time you spend on research to the position you are aiming for.

List what you'd like to know about a specific job ahead of the interview.

USEFUL LINKS

- **Bloomberg:** www.bloomberg.com
- **Directgov:** www.direct.gov.uk
- **Forrester Research:** www.forrester.com
- **Hoovers Company Info:** www.hoovers.com
- **JobSearch:** www.jobsearch.co.uk
- **Keynote:** www.keynote.co.uk

6

Job-hunting online

The Internet has completely changed the job-search process, and savvy job hunters use the Web as a mine of information. Now that your CV and covering letter are ready to go, think about how you can get the best from the Internet in your job search.

STEP ONE BE AWARE OF THE OPPORTUNITIES WHATEVER YOUR TARGET JOB MARKET

The Internet isn't useful only for searching for high-tech jobs. In fact, organisations of all types and sizes use their websites to post information about job openings and have systems in place to interact with candidates who are using the Web for job hunting. This trend did begin with high-tech industries, but has now spread to most kinds of businesses. Recruitment websites such as Monster, Jobsite, and Total Jobs (to name but a few) that allow you to post your CV online so that recruiters can even come to you direct. If appropriate, you can create a video CV, where people can see you talking about your skills and experience. This won't be appropriate for everyone, of course, but for some roles (particularly where selling or persuasive skills are needed), can help grab attention.

STEP TWO DO THE GROUNDWORK

1 Be clear about the kind of job you want, and the kind of company you would like to work for

Refresh your memory about your career objective, identify your marketable skills, and choose the right type of CV before you get online. The Web is a huge resource and if you are not completely clear and focused about what you are looking for, you could waste countless hours clicking about.

If your goal is to work in a high-tech organisation, in a job that requires Internet knowledge and skills, then you will need to demonstrate your abilities in your approach, particularly in the choices you make about the way you present your CV.

2 Choose which format or formats you will use

for your CV The list below details some of the various types of format you can use for CVs. If you're applying for an advertised vacancy, the advertisement will normally specify the format that the company prefers, but if you're hoping to make a speculative application to a business, contact them first to see what suits them best. If you send in a CV in a format that they can't open easily (if at all!), you'll be making your job search a lot harder for yourself.

TOP TIP!

There are literally thousands of websites offering job vacancies online, so knowing what you want to do really will cut down on the amount of time you'll have to spend sifting through them.

- **Word document CV.** Unlike those sent in a text format, CVs prepared in Word will retain all the formatting you have selected. Again, these are easy to e-mail.

- **PDF CV.** If you have the appropriate software, you can turn your CV into a pdf (portable document format) file, a compact way of enabling you to integrate text, illustrations, and colour into an e-mailable document.

- **Web-based CV.** A non-traditional CV that is posted on your website. Typically, it is not just a posting of your CV but instead breaks up the document into several components such as work experience, specialised skills, education, and references. Each of these topics could have content on a separate page.

- **CD-ROM CV.** Less common than the formats above, this type of CV that typically incorporates a multimedia presentation of your skills and qualifications for a particular position. The CV is burned onto a CD-ROM and posted to the potential employer.

STEP THREE GET ONLINE

1 Use the Internet to target potential employers and to get relevant information . . .

Begin your search by using one of the search engines such as Google or Yahoo, or one of the Internet employer databases listed at the end of this action list. Make a list of your criteria so that you can narrow your search. Most databases are organised by industry type, organisation size, and location. These categories can help you to eliminate large numbers of potential employers.

Once you have a list of potential employers, you can begin to screen them by visiting their websites. These may be in the database, or can be found through a search engine.

2 . . . or to register your CV with a recruitment agency

Many recruitment agencies or career-related websites now offer an online service to both job hunters and companies trying to fill a vacancy. For job hunters, registering your CV online is a quick and easy process, and means that should an interesting vacancy arise, you can ask the agency to submit your CV quickly.

In addition, take advantage of e-mail job alerts, in which agencies or career websites e-mail you when a job that meets your specifications comes on the market. This is another quick and easy way to keep on top of job opportunities in your particular market and it will also give you an idea of which companies are expanding or starting up.

TOP TIP!
If you do register for e-mail alerts, don't register your current work e-mail address. Use your personal e-mail.

3 Keep a log of potential employers

Create your own database of organisations you are targeting, and keep track of information you have gathered about each. You don't need a complicated computer package to do this: use Excel if you have it or set up a table in Word. Whatever you use, you'll be able to record any job-search actions you take for each organisation, such as dates of letters and CVs you have sent, what form of CV you used, dates of phone calls, and who you spoke to and what was said.

4 Network

Networking is one of the best ways of getting a new job and finding out about potential openings. The Internet has revolutionised the way that people can keep in touch with each other, and one of the simplest ways to use it for networking is to e-mail people on your contact list. You can ask them about industry trends, potential job openings, or for specific contacts within an organisation. Other ways of networking on the Web include:

- **Social networking sites.** LinkedIn and Facebook are just two popular sites that allow you to get in touch with prospective employers or contacts.

- **Blogs.** If you have a blog and a good amount of regular visitors, you could flag up your job search there (but do run the risk of your present employer finding out).

- **E-mail lists or listservs.** This is a way of sending a simple e-mail to a large number of people. When someone responds to your e-mail, everyone on the list receives the message. This is useful for asking questions about what is going on in a particular field or industry, or to get information about an organisation. Most listservs do not encourage direct job searches. It's best to participate in the listserv for a couple of weeks before you post any messages, so that you get a feel for what is acceptable.

- **Chat rooms or bulletin boards.** These are an excellent way to network in real-time on the Web. Chat rooms are websites that allow several people to communicate interactively using text messages. If you find chat rooms that are based on your professional interests, you are likely to meet people who can provide you with valuable information and possible leads.

As with all other types of networking, though, remember to:

- Thank people for their time and help when they get back to you.

- Offer your help to other people as much as you possibly can.

- Be patient.

5 Create your own Web page

You don't have to be a techie to create a Web page. These days, all the major Internet Service Providers (ISPs) offer free or inexpensive Web pages to their subscribers. If your ISP does not offer this service, you can get free Web pages on www.geocities.com (currently owned by Yahoo), which are created by choosing simple templates and adding your own text. They are quick and easy and will provide some basic information about you. You can include your photo and your CV. Depending on your professional background, you may want to include samples of your work or articles you have written in your specialist field.

TOP TIP!
Domain names can be bought very cheaply now, and doing a quick search for sites that offer this service will pull up a whole host of options. Remember to check that you're not being stung for any hidden charges before you go ahead and buy, however.

If you are seeking a high-tech job or a creative position in the arts or advertising, you may want to purchase your own domain name and create a more complex and sophisticated website that could include video, audio, art, photos, and whatever else you think will best portray your skills and abilities to potential employers.

Remember to include your e-mail address and website address on all correspondence, in e-mail signatures, and on your business cards.

COMMON MISTAKES

YOU DON'T HAVE A CLEAR GOAL AND PLAN
If you've not taken the time to narrow your focus and to design and target a job that you would really love, you will find that you will spend hours surfing aimlessly. Many people who do this eventually

feel drained, overwhelmed, and confused, it's essential to have clearly defined goals. If you're really rusty or planning a radical change, a career consultant may be able to offer extra help (but do check the cost first).

YOUR APPROACH IS TOO CASUAL

Online interaction can be quite casual, and it is common for people to use abbreviations and not to worry about typos or misspellings in e-mails. However, if you are job hunting, you cannot afford to be slapdash. Remember that hundreds or thousands of people may see your online communications. Make them as professional as possible by using the appropriate tone, grammar, spelling, and sign-off when you.

YOU EXPECT TOO MUCH TOO SOON

Even though the Internet has speeded up the way we communicate with other people, it isn't able to speed up the time it will take you to find the right job, so don't expect miracles.

USEFUL LINKS

- **Biz/ed:** www.bized.co.uk
- **Companies House (company search facility):** www.companieshouse.gov.uk
- **Guardian Jobs:** http://jobs.guardian.co.uk
- **Hemscott:** www.hemscott.net
- **Hoover's Online UK:** www.hoovers.com/freeuk
- **iVillage:** www.ivillage.co.uk/workcareer
- **Job-page:** www.job-page.co.uk
- **Monster Careers Centre:** www.monster.co.uk
- **NewBusiness:** www.newbusiness.co.uk

7

Choosing the right first job

If you've been preparing your CV for the first time, this chapter aims to give you some help when it comes to finding the right start to your career.

Although people change jobs and indeed career directions frequently these days, it's still important to take care when you choose your first job. Sometimes it can be difficult to know whether you're aiming too low, too high, or at the wrong jobs for the wrong reasons.

As you start out on your job hunt, think about:

- **What kind of a career have you prepared yourself for?**
- **Are you financially able to hold out for the best job?**
- **How prepared are you to launch a professional job campaign?**

Why is my first job so important?

Nowadays, people very rarely work for one company for the entirety of their working life; in fact, the average person works for seven or more companies in their lifetime.

When you are looking for your second job, employers will base their evaluation of you on your existing job title and by the reputation of the company where you are working. It is extremely difficult to go from a low-level position at an unknown organisation into a much higher position in a well-known organisation. On the other hand, it is much easier to go from a good professional position at a well-known company into a better professional position at an even more successful organisation. All in all, then, a good first job can often make it easier for you to climb the ladder in your chosen field.

What if I want to work in a non-profit organisation?

It doesn't matter: your first job is still important. There is a hierarchy in the voluntary sector in terms of prestige, power, status, and success, just as there is in the private sector. This hierarchy may not influence career choices so heavily, but it still has an effect. Ideally, you are better off establishing your career by working for a well-known and successful voluntary organisation than by working for a relatively unknown and unconnected organisation. If you truly want to have a positive impact on the world (which is most people's motivation for working in a voluntary organisation), you are probably better off if you can do that in an organisation with resources and clout.

What key question should I be asking myself?

The million-dollar question is 'Do I want to be a specialist or a generalist?' If you have chosen a particular field to pursue (such as biology, engineering, finance, music, or nursing) that you are really passionate about, then you probably are a specialist. If, on the other hand, you are interested in eventually becoming an organisational leader or an entrepreneur, you are probably more of a generalist. As a specialist, you would want to choose a first job that allows you in time to progress further in your field. As a generalist, you would want to choose a first job that will offer you opportunities to learn more about other fields, and to develop your leadership abilities.

STEP ONE WRITE A 'WORK PURPOSE STATEMENT'

The following useful exercise is adapted from Zen and the Art of Making a Living by Laurence G Boldt (Arkana, 1999):

Complete each of the following sentences:

- The way I want to contribute is . . .
- The people I want to serve are . . .
- The scale I want to work at is . . . (for example, individual, community, national, global).

Now combine these sentences into one statement about your work purpose that includes who you want to serve, the way you want to serve them, and the scope of the impact you want to make.

STEP TWO EXPLORE

1 Think about potential career roles

Make a list of at least ten different career roles that would be compatible with your 'Work Purpose Statement'. Now select the three that are most interesting to you.

2 Learn about the lifestyle associated with each

Use the Internet and personal contacts (if possible) to get a better understanding of what it would be like to work in each of these potential career roles. Find out what a typical day is like for someone who does that job so you know what it's really like.

STEP THREE ASSESS YOUR FINANCIAL SITUATION AND YOUR TIMESCALE

Work out how long you have to find your first job. If you don't have the financial support to wait for the 'perfect' first job, then decide on your minimum criteria for accepting a position. These criteria could be related to finance, working conditions, or geographic location, for example. At the very least, if you are accepting a job that does not fit your 'work purpose', then be sure that it gives you the time and opportunity to keep looking for a better position.

STEP FOUR START APPLYING

Follow the steps outlined in chapters one to six to find out how to research the job market and create a professional CV and covering letter.

COMMON MISTAKES

❌ YOU CHOOSE A CAREER THAT SOMEONE ELSE THINKS YOU SHOULD PURSUE

All too often, people choose a career path that someone else, such as a parent, teacher, or lecturer thinks is right for them. Often family pressures come into play. If your grandmother and mother were both doctors, you may be expected to follow them in their chosen career path. Resist this pressure if you can, as it doesn't take into account your gifts and talents. If you want to do something else entirely, keep plugging away until you find the right job for you.

❌ YOU TAKE A JOB JUST BECAUSE IT PAYS WELL

If you are lucky enough to be offered several alternatives when you are looking for your first job, it is tempting to take the one with the best salary. When you are starting your career, this is what seems to make the most sense but it is short-term thinking. If the job does not fit your personality or your sense of purpose in life, you will either be looking for another job very quickly, or you will stay and be miserable. It's much better to take a long-term view when you accept your first job. Ask yourself how the job will help you develop your skills and help you get to your ultimate work goals.

❌ YOU JUMP AT THE FIRST OFFER

It's understandable that people take the first offer they get even if they've applied for several jobs, especially if money is tight and they're itching to move on and start the next part of their life. It is, however, often a mistake. If you do get an offer but you're not sure about accepting it, don't be afraid to ask (politely!) for a little time to think over the job offer thoroughly. Make sure you thank the employer for their offer, give them a date (say two or three days hence) when you'll get back to them, and stick to it. If you eagerly accept a position without taking a little bit of cooling-off time, you may be jumping into something when you haven't considered some of the possible pitfalls.

YOU GO TO WORK FOR A FAMILY MEMBER OR A FRIEND BECAUSE THAT'S THE EASIEST THING TO DO

Everybody expects you to join the family business. Or your parents encourage a family friend to take you on. It might seem like an easy solution to finding your first job, but doing this, unless it's what you really want, means abdicating all responsibility for yourself and putting the direction of your life and career in someone else's hands. It may be that one of these opportunities is the perfect one for you, in which case, great. Do take time to analyse and follow the steps above, though, so that you know you are making a rational and informed decision.

YOU AVOID TRYING TO FIND THE KIND OF WORK YOU WOULD REALLY LOVE, BECAUSE PEOPLE TELL YOU THAT THE JOB MARKET IS BAD OR IT'S NOT PRACTICAL

It is amazing what you can do if you are determined to make your dream come true. You can be incredibly creative and resourceful. It may be that you will have to work harder and take a little longer to move into the career you would really love to have, but it will be worth it in the long run.

STEPS TO SUCCESS

- Decide if you want to be a specialist or a generalist.
- Write a work purpose statement.
- Think about potential careers and their associated lifestyles.

- Assess your financial situation.
- Don't be hasty. Take time to come to a decision and weigh up all the advantages and disadvantages of the position.

USEFUL LINKS

- **The Job Hunter's Bible:** www.jobhuntersbible.com

Functional CV

CHRIS O'NEILL

18 Reading Road
Woking
Surrey
WO25 1LP

Phone (home) 011 6979 1975
Mobile 07960 851 796
e-mail o_neill@gmail.com

A self-motivated and hardworking sales executive with a wide variety of sales experience.

An effective communicator and enthusiastic team worker with a proven track record, I am looking for a new challenge in a position where my previous experience, sales and communication skills can be successfully put to use.

RESPONSIBLE

- I am now responsible for 10 major accounts within a busy sales environment.

- Although we are operating within an extremely competitive market, my team has consistently achieved and outperformed company sales targets. Since my arrival we have grown sales turnover year on year by an average of 30%.

- I have instigated a policy of regularly following up on lapsed accounts, which has had a success rate of 4 out of 10 customers returning to us after our telephone call.

HARDWORKING

- In each job I have done I have continued willingly to take on more responsibility and to evolve within my role.
- I can claim credit for a marked improvement in customer service. In a recent customer satisfaction survey our ratings were up from an average of 6/10 before I arrived to an average of 8/10.
- I have been involved in organising twice-yearly sales conferences to improve communication between the sales force and other company employees, as well as to enhance relations with major customers.

COMMUNICATOR

- Throughout my career I have effectively liaised with customers across a broad range of business sectors.
- I have prepared and presented quarterly and annual projections and budgets.
- The activities I do in my spare time, especially football and acting, are proof of my communication skills.

TEAM PLAYER

- I have been responsible for initiating and organising several training and morale-building days for the sales force.
- As captain of a local football team, I organised training, matches and socials. Under my guidance, the team won more games than they lost during the season – for the first time ever!

- I am a member of the Woking Amateur Dramatics Society. With so many busy members, it is quite a feat of organisation and teamwork to produce such enjoyable twice-yearly events.

Employment

2003 – present	*BT*
2007 – present	Senior Accounts Manager
2005 – 2007	Accounts Manager
2003 – 2005	Senior Sales Assistant
2001 – 2003	*Prudential*
2002 – 2003	Sales Assistant
2001 – 2002	Administrative Assistant

Training

General IT, including specific training in Excel, Access, Word and Powerpoint
Presentation Skills, Negotiation Skills, Effective Time Management, Teamworking
First Aid

Qualifications and Education

2:2 BA (Hons), Business Studies from University of East Anglia A-Levels: Business Studies (B), Politics (B), Chemistry (C) GCSEs: 1 A, 7 Bs, 1 C

Personal Details

Date of Birth	19 November 1979
Marital Status	single
Interests	football, cinema, golf, amateur dramatics and reading
Current salary	£35,000 + performance-related bonus + benefits

Speculative Chronological CV

JOSEPHINE CATTERALL

5a Hanton Street,
London,
SE13 1DF

Tel: (020) 8868 9854
Mobile: (07914) 248553
E-mail: jfcatterall@hotmail.com

OBJECTIVE

To become a HR generalist manager with a leadership role within a blue-chip environment. I am looking for a challenging position that will involve managing resourcing, development, and employee relations issues in the United Kingdom or internationally.

EMPLOYMENT HISTORY

Nov 2007– present **HR Organisational Development Advisor (Latin America), GP International Trading and Shipping Company Ltd**

Duties:

To identify and solve organisational effectiveness problems within GP International and to establish close working relationships with both clients and a network of change experts. This provides advice that will increase the effectiveness of the client's organisation and at the same time produce alignment with the main elements of the Latin America cultural change plan.

Achievements:

- Contributed to the formulation and implementation of the Latin

America cultural change plan, especially in areas related to: organisation design and effectiveness.

- Co-ordinated learning activities with a strong link to changing culture or related to collective and organisational development, such as: change management programme, coaching for performance, and creating winning teams.

Jan 2006–Oct 2007 **Human Resources Policy Adviser, GP International Trading and Shipping Company Ltd**

Duties:
To provide professional advice on all HR policy matters including reward and recognition, employee relations, development, and resourcing, and to develop UK policy and implement policy changes within the business.

Achievements:
- Developed an equal opportunities policy and good practice guidance framework for GP companies in the UK, which has enhanced its legislative compliance and understanding amongst staff and management.

- Revised the Career Break policy in conjunction with the policy committee.

- Advised HR colleagues on several employee relations issues including providing employment law advice on disciplinary, grievance, and poor performance issues.

May 2003–Dec 2005 **Human Resources Adviser, GP International Trading and Shipping Company Ltd**

Duties:

To provide front-line, operational advice to 3 distinct entities of the Global Businesses group: Marine Products, Shipping, and Aviation.

Achievements:

- Coached line managers on how to manage disciplinary, flexible working arrangements, career break, and poor performance processes.
- Ran several internal and external recruitment processes through all stages from advert design and placement to candidate selection.
- Designed and delivered Data Protection Act workshop for the HR department.

Sept 2001–May 2003 **Human Resources Business Partner, GP U.K. Exploration and Production**

Duties:

Provided business-focused advice on a range of issues, including the four main areas of HR (reward, development, employee relations, and resourcing) and specifically helped to manage a large-scale redundancy exercise.

Achievements:

- Part of an HR team responsible for delivering approximately 100 position reductions as part of a cost-reduction exercise.
- Acted as staff consultative committee HR representative and secretary — delivered negotiating skills training and team-building

workshops to staff reps to improve the quality of their participation.

Education

2000–2001	Postgraduate Diploma in French, McGill University, Montreal, Canada
1997–2000	BA (Hons) Experimental Psychology, University of Bristol
1996–1997	A Levels: Biology (A), French (A), German (B), St Stephen's School, Ely, Cambs

Professional Qualifications

2005–2007	MSc in Employee Relations, University of Westminster, London
2003–2004	Graduate of the Chartered Institute of Personnel and Development

Where to find more help

GLOBAL RÉSUMÉ AND CV GUIDE

Mary Anne Thompson

John Wiley, 2000 288pp ISBN: 0471380768

This book uses an international approach to creating CVs that will be of interest to anyone hoping to work overseas. Experts from over 40 countries provide cultural do's and don'ts, information on business practices, and job-hunting tips that will help you create a CV tailored to the specific requirements of a target country. Standard coverage for each country includes a country overview, CV specifics, CV presentation, cover letters, job-information sources, websites, and interview advice.

HOW TO GET A JOB YOU'LL LOVE: A PRACTICAL GUIDE TO UNLOCKING YOUR TALENTS AND FINDING YOUR IDEAL CAREER 5TH ED

John Lees

McGraw-Hill Professional, 2008 256pp ISBN: 9780077121808

This book is aimed at anyone about to embark on a job search. Containing a range of exercises to help the reader find out where his or her talents really lie, the book will appeal to people looking for their first job as well as those already on their career path.

CAN I CHANGE YOUR MIND? THE CRAFT AND ART OF PERSUASIVE WRITING

Lindsay Camp

A & C Black, 2007 256pp ISBN: 9780713678499

Being able to argue a case in writing is a must for all job-seekers and in this book, Lindsay Camp shows how it's done. Of particular use is the chapter on the 'new' 3Rs: reader, response, and result.

Index

achievements, reviewing experiences 15
agencies:
- covering letters 43
- e-mail job alerts 65
- Internet applications 45
- registering CVs with 65

annual reports, researching job market 53

biographies 11
blog 66
Boldt, Laurence G. 72
brainstorming, targeted CVs 26
bullet points 38
'busy' CVs 40

capabilities CVs 22, 24, 27, 29
career advisers 68
career breaks 14, 37
career history 33
career objectives 10, 33
- choosing first jobs 69
- common mistakes 18, 74
- comparing skills with 17

career roles, choosing first jobs 74
carers, career breaks 14
CD-ROM CVs 64
chat rooms 66
chronological CVs 22, 23, 29
companies:
- choosing first jobs 69
- online job hunting 61
- researching job market 53

computer spellcheckers 38
contact information 33
cooling-off time, job offers 76
covering letters 43
- common mistakes 50
- customising 50
- drafting 46
- following up 29
- hand-written 39
- importance of 45
- length 48
- templates 50

customising:
- covering letters 50
- CVs 37

CVs (curriculum vitae):
- capabilities CVs 22, 24, 27, 29
- chronological CVs 22, 23, 29
- common mistakes 28
- fitting to situation 24
- following up 39
- formats 63
- functional CVs 22, 25, 29
- gaps in 37
- layout 36
- length 32
- ordering information 33
- printed CVs 37

real purpose 8
- selecting CV type 32
- speculative CVs 9
- targeted CVs 9, 22, 26

types of 21
updating 40
writing 36

databases:
of potential employers 65
domain names 67
drafting covering letters 46

e-mail:
addresses 33
CV formats 63
job alerts 65
networking 66
Economist website 55
education 33
capabilities CVs 28
chronological CVs 25
functional CVs 26
listing achievements 35
reviewing experiences 12
targeted CVs 27
employees, researching job market 57
envelopes, covering letters 50
experiences:
biography 11, 19
professional experience 35
reviewing 12, 18

Facebook 65
family:
career breaks 14, 37
and career paths 74
financial situation, choosing first jobs 74
Financial Times website 55
first jobs, choosing 69
follow up phone calls 29, 39
fonts:
covering letters 50
CVs 38, 40, 63
type size 38, 40
formats:
CVs 38
online CVs 63
functional CVs 22, 23, 25, 29

gaps in CV 37
generalists, choosing first jobs 66
goals:
career objectives 10, 17, 33
identifying 7
online job hunting 67
Google 64
grammar 38, 49, 68

hand-written CVs 39

hobbies 13, 36

industry trends, researching job market 54, 58
information:
'busy' CVs 40
career history 33
contact information 33
education 33, 35
ordering 33
researching job market 53
Internet:
job applications via 45
networking 65
online job hunting 61
researching job market 55
search engines 64
web pages 67
Internet Service Providers (ISPs) 67
interpersonal skills 17
interviews, suggesting in covering letters 48

inventory, skills 15

job descriptions 57
job market, researching 53

key skills see *skills*

layout 41
leisure interests 13, 36
letters *see* covering letters
libraries, researching job market 47, 55
lifestyle, and career roles 74
lists, bullet points 38

marketable skills *see* skills

networking 66
non-profit organisations 71
notice period 51

offers, deciding whether to accept 75
online job hunting 61
overselling yourself 41

paper:
- covering letters 49
- printed CVs 38, 63

pdf CVs 63
phone calls, follow up 29, 39
printed CVs 38, 63
professional experience 35
proofreading 38, 49

qualifications:
- covering letters 48
- CVs 35, 36

reality checks 17, 19
recruitment agencies *see* agencies
redundancy 38
references 36
rejections, coping with 29
research:
- chosen companies 56
- common mistakes 58
- industry trends 55, 58
- job market 53
- online job hunting 63
- specific jobs 57
- writing covering letters 47

salary 51, 74
scannable CVs 63
search engines 64
skills:
- identifying key skills 7, 9
- leisure activities 13
- 'skills inventory' 15

social networking sites 66
specialists, choosing first jobs 71
speculative CVs 9
spellcheckers 38
spelling errors 38, 49, 68
sport 13, 36
stationery 38

targeted CVs 9, 22, 26
technical skills, 'skills inventory' 15
templates:
- covering letters 50
- CVs 38
- web pages 67

timescale, choosing first jobs 74
training, 'skills inventory' 15
travel 36, 38
typefaces:
- covering letters 49
- CVs 38, 41, 63
- type size 38, 41

UK Trade and Investment website 55
unemployment 38
updating CVs 41

video CV 63
voluntary work:
 career breaks 14
 choosing first jobs 71

web pages 67
websites:
 chat rooms 66
 e-mail job alerts 64
 newsgroups 66
 online job hunting 63
 researching job market 55, 56
 Web-based CVs 64
Word document CVs 64
work experience 13, 33
writing CVs 36

Yahoo 64